# Soul-Winning 101

## A Practical Guide to
## Free Grace Evangelism

## Matthew Correll

# Contents

*The fruit of the righteous is a tree of life; and he that winneth souls is wise.* —Proverb 11:30.

# Preface

The world is a horrible place, sin-stricken, pervasively wicked, a cesspool of pestilence. Ephesians 5:16. 1 John 5:18. The Gospel is the greatest news that ever existed anyway you look at it. The world needs this message more than anything. To wit: God came down in the flesh in the form of His perfect Son, Jesus Christ to painfully die on the cross for the sins of the whole world. 1 John 2:2. He was buried and rose again to freely save us by His grace. We receive the free gift of eternal life by faith alone in Christ alone. John 3:16. Romans 5:1. Ephesians 2:5-9.

So to rectify how wicked this planet is why not spend as much time as possible telling people about this Good News.

2 Thessalonians 3:1.

*Finally, brethren, pray for us, that the word of the Lord may have free course, and be glorified, even as it is with you.*

I am writing this so that by, the grace of God, Christians may be more equipped in sharing this wondrous Good News to others.

I hope and pray that you thoroughly enjoy this book and that your soul-winning experience will be maximized.

God bless.

# 1 – Who Is Jesus Christ?

Before we delve into the subject of evangelism, I felt it was important that we know who Jesus Christ is at an epistemic level and exactly why we should tell others about Him with detail as we evangelize. I will let the Bible speak for itself on this subject.

Who is Jesus Christ?

1. He is coequal with God.

John 10:30.

*I and my Father are one.*

2. He is God's uniquely born Son.

1 Corinthians 1:9.

*God is faithful, by whom ye were called unto the fellowship of his Son Jesus Christ our Lord.*

3. He is the only way or means of salvation.

Acts 4:12.

*Neither is there salvation in any other: for there is none other name under heaven given among men, whereby we must be saved.*

4. He is the supernatural bread of life.

John 6:48.

*I am that bread of life.*

5. He is the Guarantor of eternal life.

John 6:47.

*Verily, verily, I say unto you, He that believeth on me hath everlasting life.*

6. He is and was sinlessly perfect.

Hebrews 4:15.

*For we have not an high priest which cannot be touched with the feeling of our infirmities; but was in all points tempted like as we are, yet without sin.*

7. He was born of a virgin.

Isaiah 7:14.

*Therefore the Lord himself shall give you a sign; Behold, a virgin shall conceive, and bear a son, and shall call his name Immanuel.*

8. He is the only Saviour of the world.

John 4:42.

*And said unto the woman, Now we believe, not because of thy saying: for we have heard him ourselves, and know that this is indeed the Christ, the Saviour of the world.*

9. He is the personification of eternal life and eternal hope.

1 John 5:12-13.

*He that hath the Son hath life; and he that hath not the Son of God hath not life. These things have I written unto you that believe on the name of the Son of God; that ye may know that ye have eternal life, and that ye may believe on the name of the Son of God.*

10. He is the free gift of God.

Romans 6:23.

*For the wages of sin is death; but the gift of God is eternal life through Jesus Christ our Lord.*

11. He is the resurrection and the life.

John 11:25-26.

*Jesus said unto her, I am the resurrection, and the life: he that believeth in me, though he were dead, yet shall he live: And whosoever liveth and believeth in me shall never die. Believest thou this?*

12. He is the demonstrator of God's agape love.

Romans 5:8.

*But God commendeth his love toward us, in that, while we were yet sinners, Christ died for us.*

13. He is the Lord.

Luke 2:11.

*For unto you is born this day in the city of David a Saviour, which is Christ the Lord.*

1 John 5:20 describes the real Jesus Christ.

*And we know that the Son of God is come, and hath given us* an understanding, that we may know him that is <u>true</u>, and we are in him that is <u>true</u>, even in his Son Jesus Christ. This is the <u>true</u> God, and eternal life.

2 Corinthians 11:3-4... describes a false christ.

But I fear, lest by any means, as the serpent beguiled Eve through his subtilty, so your minds should be corrupted from the simplicity that is in Christ. For if he that cometh preacheth another Jesus, whom we have not preached, or if ye receive another spirit, which ye have not received, or another gospel, which ye have not accepted, ye might well bear with him.

Here is a dichotomy showing the comparative differences between the real Christ and the false christs.

| Real Christ vs. | False Christ |
|---|---|
| 1. Saviour of the world. John 4:42. | 1. Savior of only the elect. |
| 2. Died for all sins. 1 John 1:7. | 2. Died only for past sins. |
| 3. Paid it all. John 19:30. | 3. Needs our surrendering to his lordship. |
| 4. Gives eternal life as a gift. Romans 6:23. | 4. It will cost you your life. |
| 5. Eternally secures us. John 10:28. | 5. Loses us and damns us if we sin. |
| 6. Is the only way to heaven. Acts 4:12. | 6. Adopts another man's name. (Calvin). |
| 7. Saves believers instantaneously. John 5:24. | 7. Makes us persevere to the end. |

As evangelists, we unrelentingly need to tell others who the real Jesus Christ is because many false christs are out there with a false gospel. 2 Corinthians 11:3-4, Galatians 1:6-9.

God bless.

# 2 – Simplest Plan of Salvation

Finding a plan of salvation that is simple and clear may be quite the task due to the pervasion of false doctrine that plagues the Internet, our scholastic textbooks and church pulpits the world over. Satan is working overtime in corrupting the simple truth and thus complicating it. (Luke 8:12, 2 Corinthians 11:3-4.)

In fact, to even find a good, biblically sound tract nowadays is few and far between. So many tracts are anything but simple and clear. Much heretical lingo seems to crop up in a majority of gospel presentations way too often. More often than not unfortunately.

Here is a list of this confusing rhetoric.

1. Repent of your sins.
2. Promise to serve God.
3. Submit to the Lordship of Christ.
4. Be willing to forsake your former lifestyle.
5. Commit your life to Christ.
6. Be willing to obey and follow Christ.
7. Give Christ control over your life.

And this is just a short litany of all the various verbiage I've read on tracts and or heard false teachers say to their congregants in order to veritably confuse them on this crucial gospel subject.

The gospel was never meant to be like this. It is a wonderfully simple message that even a child can readily understand.

Matthew 18:1-6. 2 Timothy 3:15. Mark 9:42.

Luke 18:16-17.

*But Jesus called them unto him, and said, Suffer little children to come unto me, and forbid them not: for of such is the kingdom of God. Verily I say unto you, Whosoever shall not receive the kingdom of God as a little child shall in no wise enter therein.*

A child does not and cannot understand all this aforementioned, confounding rhetoric. But they can however understand the concept of believing on Christ to forever save them and take them to heaven when they die. Acts 16:31, John 3:16.

As soul-winners; it is incumbent to get the gospel out clearly and with childlike simplicity.

For instance: God sent His Son, Jesus Christ to die on the cross for your sins. He was buried and rose again on the third day. This was how He divinely purchased your way into heaven. Eternal life is a free gift entirely by God grace. (Romans 5:15.)

You receive this gift by simply believing in Jesus for it. John 3:36.

*He that believeth on the Son hath everlasting life: and he that believeth not the Son shall not see life; but the wrath of God abideth on him.*

Some may be thinking: "that's it." I just have to believe in Jesus and then I am saved and going to heaven no matter what I do. It can't be that easy! That's just too simple.

But it really is that simple.

Jesus did the difficult part when He took a brutal beating and ultimately died on the cross to fully satisfy the wrath of God and ultimately pay for our sins. (Isaiah 50:6.)

Your response is very simple. Just receive by faith alone what He did for you and you are eternally saved and secure forever. (John 6:58.) No strings attached. It was never meant to be a complicated message. The Gospel really is Good News and it is so good that even a very young child can readily understand it.

We are all sinners. Romans 3:23, 5:12. Galatians 3:22.

Jesus is the only Saviour. Luke 2:11. 1 Timothy 2:5.

We receive the free gift of eternal life by faith alone in Christ alone or (simply believing). Romans 5:1. John 3:16. 1 John 5:1.

I will not apologize for the simplicity of salvation by grace through faith alone in Christ alone but will openly proclaim it whenever possible.

The first step in becoming an effective soul-winner is to have the simplest plan of salvation possible.

Romans 12:8.

*Or he that exhorteth, on exhortation: he that giveth, let him do it with simplicity; he that ruleth, with diligence; he that sheweth mercy, with cheerfulness.*

Here is a very simple way to present the gospel.

### The Simple Gospel way to heaven.

God sent His Son, Jesus Christ to die on the cross for your sins. He was buried and rose again to save you from hell and give you the free gift of eternal life. Rom 6:23. 5:8.

You receive eternal life by believing in Jesus.

The Bible says.
Acts 16:31. Believe on the Lord Jesus Christ and thou shalt be saved and thy house.

Jesus said in John 6:47. Verily, verily, I say unto you, He that believeth on me hath everlasting life.

Once saved, always saved.
John 10:28. And I give unto them eternal life and they shall NEVER perish.

Do you believe that just by simply believing in Jesus you have everlasting life. Yes___ or No___.

I hope you enjoy the following subsets.

# 3 – Calvinism: The Enemy of Soul-Winning

One of the biggest adversaries of soul-winning is this demonic doctrine called: Calvinism. Calvinism in a nutshell is the false idea that God has pre-selected who would be saved and who would be damned from eternity past thus giving them no choice or chance (to receive grace) in the matter whatsoever. It's pure damnable heresy!

Calvinism is totally contrary to many scriptures.

(John 5:40. Hebrews 4:1-2. Revelation 22:17, Revelation 3:20. 21:6. Acts 14:16. John 3:18. John 1:7. Deuteronomy 30:19. Acts 28:27.)

Calvinism is so evil that it renders people so dead in their sins that they can't even believe the gospel let alone respond to any other light God reveals. (John 12:36.) But if this concept were true then the Gospel of John shouldn't have been penned for the sole purpose of John was to tell sinful people that believing in Jesus as the Christ resulted in eternal life through His Name. John 20:31.

The truth of the matter is that anyone, through the aegis of the Holy Ghost and the power of the gospel, can believe on Christ. John 1:7-9. John 4:10. John 3:16. Romans 1:16. John 6:44. Romans 10:17. 1 Corinthians 1:18-21.)

According to Calvinism only those who God elected (so-called regenerated) will believe and the rest will remain in unchanged spiritual blindness forevermore. This is why Calvinism is such an enemy to soul-winning? If Christ didn't die for everyone but only the elect; then you can't honestly proclaim the gospel to all people for it wouldn't even apply to all people and would be deceptive at best unless to the non-elect.

However, the Bible says it applies to all people. Mark 16:15.

*And he said unto them, Go ye into all the world, and preach the gospel to every creature.*

Luke 2:30-31.

*For mine eyes have seen thy salvation, which thou hast prepared before the face of all people.*

1 Timothy 2:4.

*Who will have all men to be saved, and to come unto the knowledge of the truth.*

Why would God prepare the way of salvation for ALL people if they couldn't ALL be saved?

Furthermore why would God proclaim that He takes no pleasure in people perishing if in fact He foreordained some (perhaps many) to perish without any divine recourse?

Ezekiel 33:11.

*Say unto them, As I live, saith the Lord God, I have no pleasure in the death of the wicked; but that the wicked turn from his way and live: turn ye, turn ye from your evil ways; for why will ye die, O house of Israel?*

2 Peter 3:9.

*The Lord is not slack concerning his promise, as some men count slackness; but is longsuffering to us-ward, not willing that any should perish, but that all should come to repentance.*

John 3:17.

*For God sent not his Son into the world to condemn the world; but that the world through him might be saved.*

If God wanted people to perish in hell then He wouldn't have bothered to send His Son Jesus Christ to die on the cross and be horribly tortured to pay for their sins, yet the Bible says He did. (John 1:29. Matthew 20:19, Romans 6:9-10.)

So what kind of a message would someone who believes in this Calvinistic garbage really be telling the lost? Here is a pithy dialogue between a Calvinist and a lost person.

"Jesus might have died for you. If in fact you are one of the 'chosen elect.' You don't know if you are the elect and can only hope God chose you before the foundation of the world. That's the best you can do is hope ... eternal life is mere wishful thinking or a pipedream."

Now, I know most Calvinists will object to this so-called caricature of what they believe and teach and will retort back with something akin to this:

"We don't know who the elect are and should just preach the gospel to all people just in case."

But that is completely dishonest. If Christ didn't die for all as they fallaciously assert then it would be a patent lie to tell them He did. Telling the non-elect that Christ died for them would give them a false sense of hope if Calvinism were in fact true. Thank God it is not true and nothing more than a diabolical lie straight out of hell!

Jesus died for all people. Period!
(2 Corinthians 5:14-15. Hebrews 2:9. John 3:16. John 4:42. 1 Timothy 2:6. 1 John 2:2. 1 Timothy 2:4. 1 Timothy 4:10. Romans 5:6-8. Galatians 3:28. 1 John 4:14. Matthew 28:19, Acts 17:30. Luke 2:10-11.)

Conclusion: Calvinism is satanic garbage and is a complete hindrance to real soul-winning. We should tell people that Jesus Christ died for their sins--all of them, He was buried and rose again and that if they will simply believe on Him alone they will be eternally saved by God's marvelous grace. Ephesians 2:5.

It's not a matter of us trusting in our freewill to save us as the brainwashed Calvinists foolishly say. It is simply a matter of us taking God up on His offer of eternal life as a free gift. He is not a respecter of persons (Romans 2:11, Acts 10:34.) Jesus died for everyone and offers the free gift of eternal life to everyone equally. (Revelation 22:17. Luke 2:30-31. Luke 4:18.)

John 4:10.

*Jesus answered and said unto her, If thou knewest the gift of God, and who it is that saith to thee, Give me to drink; thou wouldest have asked of him, and he would have given thee living water.*

Revelation 21:6.

*And he said unto me, It is done. I am Alpha and Omega, the beginning and the end. I will give unto him that is athirst of the fountain of the water of life freely.*

Acts 16:30-31.

*And brought them out, and said, Sirs, what must I do to be saved? And they said, Believe on the Lord Jesus Christ, and thou shalt be saved, and thy house.*

If the god of Calvinism were the God of the Bible then the avid soul-winner would be more noble, loving and admirable than their god for desiring people to be saved that were chosen to be damned without divine remedy.

That is blasphemy to the uttermost degree.

Job 4:17.

*Shall mortal man be more just than God? shall a man be more pure than his maker?*

Romans 3:4.

*God forbid: yea, let God be true, but every man a liar; as it is written, That thou mightest be justified in thy sayings, and mightest overcome when thou art judged.*

Calvinism is utterly wicked and must be arrantly rejected from our mentality in order to efficaciously win souls and proclaim the true Gospel of grace. 1 Corinthians 15:1-4. Isaiah 58:1. Romans 1:16. 1 Corinthians 9:16.

God bless.

# 4 – Limited Atonement Is a Doctrine of Devils

Take a look at how wicked and damnable the L in TULIP is. "L" stands for limited atonement. That is the idea that Christ didn't die for everyone but only for the elect or His own as they like to foolishly say.

Espousers of Limited Atonement believe on the wrong christ (2 Corinthians 11:3-4), the wrong gospel (Galatians 1:8-9.) and aren't saved according to the Bible. (2 Thessalonians 1:8-9). Jesus Christ died for everyone equally. Hebrews 2:9, Romans 5:6-8. Those that embrace Limited Atonement after reading those verses and others with the selfsame import obviously don't believe the scripture because it is foolishness to them. 1 Corinthians 2:12-14. John 8:43-47. They don't know what "all" means. They also don't believe the word "whosoever" really means what it clearly says: "whosoever." 1 John 5:1. They are blind and can't read spiritually. Thus lost. God is love (1 John 4:7-8) and He loves all people. John 3:16, Romans 5:8. The fact is God wishes for no one to perish (2 Peter 3:9) and has through the Gospel given everyone the way of salvation. Luke 2:10, 1 Corinthians 15:3-4. Romans 1:16. Acts 4:12. The fact that some perish in hell is their own dumb fault for rejecting the Good News of the Gospel. 2 Thessalonians 2:10. John 5:40. Psalm 14:1. God can't help it that some believe not. John 3:18. Everyone is savable and those who believe on Christ are eternally saved. Acts 16:30-31.

Limited atonement posits that Jesus only died for some and only some can and will be saved and it is against their will which negates the Bible's clear teaching of: "whosoever will" Revelation 22:17. Revelation 21:6, John 4:10. Romans 10:13. Jesus said, in John 5:40: You will not come to me that you might have life. Not "cannot" but: "will not" That is what a

Calvinist who champions limited atonement has done. They have not come to the real Christ and thus they are still unsaved and going to hell. That is if that is what they've always believed.

The true gospel presentation is this. God sent His Son, Jesus Christ to die for your sins. Yours, mine and everyone's. He was buried and rose again. He gives eternal life as a free gift (Romans 6:23) to anyone who realizes they are lost, deserves to go to hell and then simply believes in Him for it. John 6:47. Not only does a limited atonement proponent not believe this but they teach that the gift of eternal life (and most of them really don't believe it is a gift) isn't offered to everyone and how could it be in their system if the atonement is limited.

They may say something to the effect of: salvation is only for the elect that God preordained. And if that is the case then salvation is not really a gift at all. A gift must be freely received or rejected, offered to all and forced on no one!

Salvation is by grace alone through faith alone in Christ alone. Ephesians 2:8-9. Romans 4:16. Anyone after being convicted by the Holy Ghost. John 16:8-12, and after hearing the powerful message of the Gospel (Romans 10:17) can believe on Christ and be saved. John 1:7. It's not limited; but unlimited, available to all and effected perfectly to those who believe. 1 Timothy 4:10.

Jesus said in John 6:47,

*Verily, verily, I say unto you He that believeth on me hath everlasting life.*

You either have believed on Him or you haven't. Jesus also said in John 11:26, that whoever lives and believes in me shall never die. Calvinists don't believe that verse because they believe that there are people alive who can't believe. Jesus lied if they are correct because He said whoever lives and believes hence everyone alive can believe! Duh. The fact that Calvinists believe that the non-elect can't believe means they don't believe that verse. They would have to say to Jesus.

"No. We don't believe that... only the elect whom God chose

can believe."

Wrong answer! That certainly is not the answer Martha gave. She said: Yeah Lord, I believe...

Calvinists are still in unbelief and still condemned! John 3:18. Now you know the Calvinist doesn't believe the Gospel nor do they believe the words of Jesus our Lord. For if they believed that verse (John 11:26) they would no longer be a Calvinist who holds to limited atonement. So their own predilection to stay a TULIP-asserting Calvinist keeps them in unbelief and keeps them unregenerate. John 3:36. John 3:5. Luke 18:17.

Conclusion: why would anyone want to believe that Jesus didn't die for everyone unless they just hated people and want them to be irremediably cast into hell and also hate God so much that they would malign His character so horrendously? The only thing I can think of is unregeneracy and utter spiritual blindness. 2 Corinthians 4:3-4.

The bottom line is that Jesus Christ died for every human being that has ever lived and is alive today and that will ever live in the future and he freely saves (John 3:17), justifies (Romans 3:26) and gives eternal life (1 John 5:11) to all without exception that simply believe on Him. (John 3:15-16.) Hands-down. Period! Limited atonement proponents do not believe this and unless and until they do they and are headed for the lake of fire. Revelation 20:15, John 5:47.

**********************************************

Here is a summary of what limited atonement has done in terms of distorting the Bible and Gospel.

1. They redefine what "world" means. John 1:29, 4:42.
2. They think Jesus didn't die for everyone which means they have judged wrongly. 2 Corinthians 5:14-15. And believed in a false Christ. 2 Corinthians 11:3-5.
3. They fear that Jesus' blood had no effect on those who go to

hell when the truth is it did and no one goes to hell because of sin. 1 John 2:2. They go to hell because they were never born again. John 3:3, 7.

4. They can't read clear verses like 1 John 2:2, 2 Peter 2:1, Hebrews 2:9, John 3:16. This is because they are spiritually blind. 2 Corinthians 4:3-5.

5. They want Jesus to NOT have died for some which makes them hateful wretches and devoid of God-given love. 1 John 4:8.

6. Their argument is based on poor choice of rhetoric. God made salvation possible so therefore man must enact his own salvation with meritorious faith. When in reality God made salvation available and man must simply receive it by faith which is non-meritorious and perfectly Biblical. Romans 4:5, Luke 7:50, John 4:10, Revelation 22:17, John 6:47. John 7:37. John 3:16, Acts 16:31. Romans 3:22.

7. They render the gospel powerless to the so-called non-elect. Romans 1:16. If there are people that can't believe and be saved then that verse is misleading, worthless and needs to be removed from the Bible.

8. They don't believe the gospel at all. They don't believe that anyone who simply believes on Jesus has everlasting life. John 6:47. They think that those who Christ didn't die for can't believe so therefore they don't believe the promise of that verse nor do they know what "whosoever" means as stated in 1John 5:1, John 3:16, John 11:26.

9. They must think that only they are sinners if Christ only died for them. But the Bible clearly states that all are sinners: Romans 5:12, 3:23. So therefore Christ had to die for all people, yet they reject this clear teaching.

10. They can't read God's word, have no truth in them and prove to be unregenerate & going to hell. John 8:43-48.

Conclusion: a saved person shouldn't have any problem believing in unlimited atonement because how would they know that Christ even died for them if there were scores of people out there (them included) that are fatalistically not atoned for? All they would have to go by would be their futile faith but if Christ didn't atone for them even their faith would be insufficient and a meaningless act of human merit if that is all they have to go by— and what good would it be if there is nothing to have faith in like (limited atonement). And it would be meaningless ... if Christ purposely didn't die for them.

However if Christ died for everyone then one would not have to worry about their salvation and then believing Jesus died for them would give them all the assurance they needed knowing that they have a Saviour who promises eternal salvation to all who have faith alone in Christ alone. The unlimited atonement adherents can have real assurance knowing that Jesus really did take away the sin of the WORLD like the Bible clearly says: John 1:29. Whereas the limited atonement bunch could only hope with subjective wishful thinking that maybe Christ died for them and maybe their faith is valid but if it's not then they're going to hell. And this would leave them just guessing that Jesus atoned for them but such guesswork would be unstable if the God of the universe has just randomly atoned for certain people and not all.

What makes them think they're are amongst the limited atonement spectrum? It would be blind faith.

"I hope I'm atoned for."

Then as the doubts accrue they would start looking for evidence within themselves and their works to see if they bear the marks of the so-called elect. Now we have works-salvation. And I would have to submit that the limited atonement adherents are in fact going to hell having believed on another jesus.

Not the one of the Bible as found in 1 Timothy 4:10. The sad thing about these lost people is they say stuff like if God offered universal or unlimited atonement they why does anyone go to hell or how can someone go to hell if their sins are paid for? What dumb questions. Just because something is paid for in full doesn't guarantee that anyone receives it. They say that those who teach that Jesus died for everyone really teach that Jesus died for no one if no one has faith. How absurd. Jesus died for everyone and even if the whole world goes to hell, it doesn't change this fact. The death, burial and resurrection is sufficient to save everyone and anyone but they have to make a choice and this is clear in the scripture.

John 3:36.

*He that believeth on the Son hath everlasting life and he that believeth not the Son shall not see life but the wrath of God abideth on Him.*

That is the bottom line.

God bless.

# 5 – Arminianism Is an Enemy to Soul-Winning

Arminianism completely strips the Gospel of its' power. Romans 1:16. It teaches a works based salvation that threatens a believer with eternal/salvific loss if the believer sins or loses faith or doesn't endure to the end or whatever. It is a flat-out lie. Salvation is a permanent gift of God. Romans 11:29 and cannot be lost for any reason. John 18:9.

Once a Christian ... always a Christian. Once a child of God, always a child of God. (1 John 5:1, Galatians 3:26, 4:6. 1 Peter 1:2, 23, John 1:12-13, 3:3-7, 1 John 3:2. 2 Corinthians 6:18.)

I will expound more on this in future subsets. But the main reason why the Arminian heresy is such an enemy to soul-winning is because it is making Jesus a liar.

Jesus promised to all who believe in Him eternal life and made it extremely clear that they would never die (that is perish in hell). John 3:15, 17:3-4, 11:26. 10:28.

How can one proclaim the Good News of the Gospel if they aren't even sure what it is?

Saved one day... lost the next?

Imagine such a dialogue.

"Hey I'm not sure where I'm going when I die and if you will give me a few minutes of your time I can tell you how you can be unsure as to where you will go when you die as well."

"Uhhhh. I'm confused."

"You shouldn't be. I'm saved ... at least until I fall back into some grievous sin and then I will be lost again."

"Huh?"

"Yeah. You can be saved temporarily that is until you lose faith and backslide."

"No thanks. I don't want that kind of salvation."

And it wouldn't be salvation.

If you could lose your salvation (or give it back,) then John 3:16 would not be true:

John 3:16.

*For God so loved the world, that he gave his only begotten Son, that whosoever believeth in him should not perish, but have everlasting life.*

According to the Arminian heresy; one could be saved and then ... let's say 34 years later fall back into gross sin and lose his/her salvation.

John 3:16 would then have to read.

For God so loved the world, that he gave his only begotten Son, that whosoever believeth in him may perish, and have 34 years of some kind of temporary life.

No. That is not what John 3:16 says nor what it means.

*For God so loved the world, that he gave his only begotten Son, that whosoever believeth in him should not perish, but have everlasting life.*

"Everlasting" means: "everlasting." It is a God-given life in heaven that will go on forever and ever and ever and ever and ever ad infinitem.

To believe the Arminian heresy that is that salvation can be lost means you don't even know what the words: 'everlasting' or 'eternal' mean.

John 6:58.

*This is that bread which came down from heaven: not as your fathers did eat manna, and are dead: he that eateth of this bread shall live for ever.*

The whole point of soul-winning is to tell people that Jesus died for them to save them from hell and give them everlasting life in heaven simply by faith alone in Christ alone. This blasphemous heresy makes soul-winning into a misleading lie which saves no one. 1 John 5:9-11.

Arminianism needs to be rejected at all costs. The goal is to tell people how to have eternal life not some other kind of temporal life that is utterly foreign to scripture.

John 10:28.

*And I give unto them eternal life; and they shall never perish, neither shall any man pluck them out of my hand.*

Deuteronomy 32:40.

*For I lift up my hand to heaven, and say, I live for ever.*

John 6:47.

*Verily, verily, I say unto you He that believeth on me hath everlasting life.*

More will be expounded on this in my subset entitled: Eternal Security and Soul-Winning.

God bless.

# 6 – Lordship Salvation Is an Enemy to Soul-Winning

Now after having covered Calvinism and Arminianism another false teaching out there is called: Lordship Salvation. It too is an enemy to soul-winning for it garbles the Gospel as well. Calvinism says Christ only died for some. Arminianism says you can lose your salvation. Lordship salvation, well it purports that simply believing in Jesus is not enough to be saved despite the fact that the Bible says it is. Romans 1:16, John 3:16. John 6:35, 1 Timothy 1:16, John 11:40, Acts 16:31, Acts 10:43, Romans 4:24, etc ... etc.

Lordship salvation teachers are wicked and utterly blasphemous. They will add anything to faith in Jesus. Repentance, surrender, good works as proof one is saved, etc.

"You can't live like the devil" they say.

"You'll know true believers by their fruits,"

"There's no such thing as a carnal Christian"

"Good works have to be there."

"You must repent of sins."

"They don't know what grace is."

"You're an antinomian."

"If it's true faith it will produce good works."

I've heard it all and it is all garbage! Look at the following verses and see how each of them refutes Lordship Salvation.

Romans 4:5.

*But to him that worketh not, but believeth on him that justifieth the ungodly, his faith is counted for righteousness.*

The one who is trying to make Christ the Lord over his/her life is not the one who is being saved here. Rather it is the one who is not working or doing anything at all but is simply believing in

**24**

# 7 – Witnessing to Muslims

Islamic tradition is a works-based tradition where ultimately one cannot know if they will go to heaven or not. In Christianity, one is saved and guaranteed heaven based on God's grace and the finished work of Jesus Christ at the cross of Calvary. (Acts 15:11. Ephesians 2:8-9, John 19:30. Ecclesiastes 3:15. John 17:2-5. Hebrews 6:11.)

Salvation is based on what has already been done for us, not what we do in this lifetime. When witnessing to a Muslim; one must emphasize the fact that we as Bible-believing Christians know 100 percent for sure that we are going to heaven (1 John 5:13.) and that in the Islamic system one cannot ever know if they will truly go to heaven or not. Let's take a look at what Muslims claim one must do to go to heaven.

1. Make a confession of faith. A Muslim must confess, "There is no God but Allah and Mohammed is the prophet of God."
2. Pray. Muslims are supposed to pray five times a day: shortly before sunrise, midmorning, noon, mid-afternoon, and after sunset.
3. Give alms. Muslims are to give about 2.5 percent of their wealth.
4. Fast during Ramadan. For one lunar month, from sunrise to sunset, Muslims are not to allow anything to pass down their throat. (Theoretically, a good Muslim would even spit out his or her salivates.) Then from sunset to sunrise, they are allowed to eat as little or as much as they please. This is their way of developing discipline and relating to the poor. (Travelers, young children and pregnant or nursing mothers do not need to keep the fast.)
5. Make a pilgrimage to Mecca. Every Muslim who is financially

able is supposed to travel to the birthplace of Islam once in his or her lifetime.

Muslims have no guarantee of being eternally saved. They believe that all their works will be accounted for and that on Judgment Day, if your bad works outweigh your good works, you are going to hell. But if your good works outweigh your bad works, you'll "probably" go to heaven.

This is no way to live, in constant wonderment as to whether you are good enough and yet there's always this gnawing abject aura that engenders chronic fear of torment if one is not living up to some unknowable standard; and surely Muslims are not good enough at all considering they are notorious for killing and other acts of wanton brutality. Even if one is so-called living a good life; this system is still based on variable circumstances.

If one is able-bodied, able-minded and or has the right daily schedule to pray; one can obtain favor with Allah. One must also be somewhat affluent and even financially sufficient enough to make pilgrimages to Mecca.

It's entirely based on human merit and human effort unlike Christians who undergo human frailty whereupon God the provider must intervene and has provided grace for us to help us in our time of need. Hebrews 4:16.

Salvation in Islam is impossible as well as enigmatic because according to their own tenets Muslims are not inherently, genetically sinful and have no real need for redemption. But this is erroneous because the Bible makes it clear that we are all sinners who need to be saved. Romans 3:23. Romans 5:12. Galatians 3:22. 1 John 1:8.

What Muslims need is Good News.

Only Christians have this.

Salvation in Christianity is totally free because Jesus Christ paid it all. 1 John 3:5. John 19:30. The bottom line in witnessing to Muslims is to show them the hope of the Christian faith.

Jesus Christ died for everyone to freely give us eternal life in heaven. 1 Peter 1:3-4.

When witnessing to Muslims or anyone for that matter, I keep stressing the fact that eternal life is a free gift. It is harder to reject the Christian faith when you understand that a person is saved without any change of lifestyle or works and that we get eternal life freely by God's grace through faith alone in Christ alone. So keep emphasizing the freeness of salvation. It has a greater effect on the lost than one might think or know.

God bless.

# 8 – Reasons Why People Won't Evangelize

I'm writing this so that Christians will not become like this. Non-soul-winners are a plight that have epidemically vitiated the world of Christendom. Too many people just sit around at Christmas parties not asking strangers what they believe, nor do they tell them what to believe in terms of the free grace gospel. This alone is sad enough and married to this horrible idea is "they most certainly won't evangelize in more hostile environments," let alone at the gospel-friendly church party.

I call it pathetic.

The rest of the Christian world deems it as normal. Soul-winning in some churches is so rare one may be ostracized for such an endeavor. When the truth is we are to find out what people believe and then affirm them if they are correct and correct them if they are wrong or nebulous about the Gospel message.

But why is nobody doing this?

Well, first and foremost, Satan has spent in my not-so-humble opinion all of his efforts in hindering this activity amongst Christian circles. He uses sin and every other distraction known to man to keep our minds off of evangelism. Luke 8:14.

The Apostle Paul in 1 Corinthians chapter 2 started off with an exhortation to his listeners to focus on Christ and Him crucified, both extremely germane to evangelism considering that the crucifixion is the crux of the Gospel and uncannily that is where the word crux was derived from.

1 Corinthians 1:1-2.

*And I, brethren, when I came to you, came not with excellency of speech or of wisdom, declaring unto you the testimony of God. For I determined not to know any thing among you, save Jesus Christ, and him crucified.*

Paul finishes up the chapter with a similar import.

1 Corinthians 2:16.

*For who hath known the mind of the Lord, that he may instruct him? but we have the mind of Christ.*

Having the mind of Christ means always being ready to give especially through evangelism. Christ evangelized many times. John 11:25-26. John 4:10-14, John 10:38. John 4:21. So should we. 1 Corinthians 9:16.

There are many reasons why people don't. Here I will name a few reasons and explain with Bible verses why most Christians are not even thinking about winning souls. The real issue is one of spiritual growth. 1 Peter 2:1-3. Here are ten reasons that I will expound about with more detail.

***Problem***

1. Lost. 2 Corinthians 4:4.
2. Carnal. 1 Corinthians 3:1-3.
3. Ashamed of the gospel. Romans 1:16.
4. No love for the lost. 1 John 4:8.
5. Fear. 2 Timothy 1:7. 1 John 4:18.
6. Focused on worldly things. Philippians 3:19.
7. They aren't filled with the Holy Spirit. Acts 1:8.
8. They are mixed up doctrinally. Colossians 1:9.
9. Unconfessed Sin. 1 John 1:9.
10. They lack evangelistic material. Philippians 2:30.

1. If a person is lost he/she cannot share the gospel. Faith must come from another person with faith. Romans 1:17. Everything is begat after it's own kind. Genesis 1:11. Plus the gospel is hid to lost people. Hid to such a degree that they are unable to share it with others.

2 Corinthians 4:3-4.

*But if our gospel be hid, it is hid to them that are lost: In whom the god of this world hath blinded the minds of them which believe not, lest the light of the glorious gospel of Christ, who is the image of God, should shine unto them.*

2. Carnality is another impediment to soul-winning.

1 Corinthians 3:1-3.

*And I, brethren, could not speak unto you as unto spiritual, but as unto carnal, even as unto babes in Christ. I have fed you with milk, and not with meat: for hitherto ye were not able to bear it, neither yet now are ye able. For ye are yet carnal: for whereas there is among you envying, and strife, and divisions, are ye not carnal, and walk as men?*

Carnal people cannot speak about spiritual things on a spiritual level and are in desperate need of spiritual growth which is what it takes to be an effective soul-winner or even to be thinking about soul-winning.

3. People who are ashamed of the gospel will not proclaim it.
Romans 1:16.

*For I am not ashamed of the gospel of Christ: for it is the power of God unto salvation to every one that believeth; to the Jew first, and also to the Greek.*

4. No love means no soul-winning.

1 John 4:8.

*He that loveth not knoweth not God; for God is love.*

5. Fear is a big deterrent for soul-winning. It's hard to witness to people if you are afraid of them.

2 Timothy 1:7.

*For God hath not given us the spirit of fear; but of power, and of love, and of a sound mind.*

6. Worldliness is one of the biggest derailments when it comes to soul winning. One has no time to get evangelistically prepared and share their faith when they are so consumed with television, music, work, sports, trivia and other secularistic activity.

Philippians 3:19.

*Whose end is destruction, whose God is their belly, and whose glory is in their shame, who mind earthly things.*

7. A lack of Holy Spirit infilling. All believers in Christ have the Holy Spirit indwelling them, (Romans 5:5, Galatians 4:6) but not all have the Holy Spirit infilled in them. (Ephesians 5:18.)

Acts 1:8.

*But ye shall receive power, after that the Holy Ghost is come upon you: and ye shall be witnesses unto me both in Jerusalem, and in all Judaea, and in Samaria, and unto the uttermost part of the earth.*

8. Bad doctrine will not produce a soul-winner but will render one a confused non-soul-winner.

Colossians 1:9.

*For this cause we also, since the day we heard it, do not cease to pray for you, and to desire that ye might be filled with the knowledge of his will in all wisdom and spiritual understanding.*

9. Unconfessed sin separates us from God experientially but not positionally. Romans 8:38-39. This lack of fellowship makes it impossible for God to bless us. And we need to be blessed to win souls.

1 John 1:9.

*If we confess our sins, he is faithful and just to forgive us our sins, and to cleanse us from all unrighteousness.*

10. Lacking material makes it difficult to go soul-winning.

Philippians 2:30.

*Because for the work of Christ he was nigh unto death, not regarding his life, to supply your lack of service toward me.*

Here is a solution to these problems.
1. Lost. Get saved. Acts 16:31.
2. Carnal. Grow spiritually. 1 Peter 2:1-3.
3. Ashamed of the gospel. Get unashamed. Romans 1:16.
4. No love for the lost. Be concerned about souls. 1 John 3:23.
5. Afraid. Let God's love cast out fear.1 John 4:18.

6. Focused on worldly things. Grow spiritually.  1 Peter 2:1-3.
7. They aren't filled with the Holy Spirit. Feed the spirit. 1 Peter 2:1-3.
8. They are mixed-up doctrinally. Get sound in faith. 2 Peter 1:2.
9. Unconfessed Sin. Confess sins. James 5:16.
10. They lack material. Ask God through supplicatory petitions and prayers. 1 John 5:14-15. Psalm 55:1-2.

Soul winning is of so much importance that my intent in writing this and sincere prayer is that we will rectify these problems with God's word and be avid soul-winners around the clock.

God bless.

# 9 – Lordship Salvation Is Leading People to Hell

Lordship salvation in any of its many malignant forms is a demonic perversion of the true Gospel of grace. (Galatians 1:6-7.) It demands that man must do good works, repent of sins and/or surrender over to the will of God in order to be saved or prove to be saved.

However the Bible plainly says that salvation is, was and always will be by God's grace alone through faith alone in Jesus Christ alone. Romans 4:16. Acts 15:11. Acts 10:43. Jesus is the Saviour. John 3:17. John 4:42, 1 John 4:14, Luke 2:11. He died, was buried and rose again to give us eternal life through faith alone in Him alone. 1 Corinthians 15:3-4, Romans 5:1. But that is NOT what Lordship Salvation teaches. They want to add many things to what Christ did which is blasphemy. And they love to qualify what so-called true faith is instead of just letting the Bible define faith. Hebrews 11:1.

Look at some of the ramifications of this false gospel of Lordship Salvation. If Lordship salvation were true; then we would be left with the following...

1. Eternal rejection from Christ at Judgment day. Matthew 7:21-23.

2. No real justification. Romans 4:5. Romans 3:28. Galatians 2:16.

3. A cancellation of eternal hope. Galatians 3:17-18.

4. A cancellation of grace. Romans 11:6. Galatians 2:21.

6. A cancellation of faith. Romans 4:13-14. 1 Corinthians 15:2.

6. No assurance. 1 John 5:13. Romans 4:16. John 6:69.

7. Boasting and bragging in front of God. Romans 4:2.

8. Self-righteousness. Luke 18:9.

9. Works salvation. Titus 3:6. 2 Timothy 1:9.

10. Another Jesus. 2 Corinthians 11:3-5.

11. A false, accursed gospel. Galatians 1:6-9.
12. A place in (HELL) the lake of fire. Revelation 20:13-15.
13. A divine blinding by God. Romans 11:7-8.
14. A rejection from Paul and Barnabas. Acts 13:46.
15. A denial of simple faith alone in Christ alone. Acts 16:31. John 3:16. Luke 7:50. 1 John 5:4-5.

Conclusion: Lordship Salvation is the natural conclusion that is derived from unsaved (lost) people who have no truth in them (Isaiah 8:20, John 5:38.) and cannot understand the spiritual things of God. 1 Corinthians 2:12-14. Matthew 13:9-13. Revelation 3:13, 22. Those who possess the Holy Spirit are children of God. Romans 8:9. And they should know that salvation is by grace alone through faith alone in the finished work of Christ alone. Plus nothing. Minus nothing. John 19:30. Once saved, always saved. John 6:37-40.

They also should understand that Lordship salvation is nothing more than a works-based salvation that is sadly leading people straight to hell! Matthew 7:22-23. Keep in mind that those who are saved by grace through faith and who have lapsed into this heresy aren't lost but unfortunately most who embrace this heresy have never been saved to begin with and can only hear the voice of Satan and not God. John 8:43-47.

God bless.

# 10 – Hand Evangelism

(Prefatory note.)
Use non-permanent markers and use black-SIN, brown-cross, red-blood.

One can tell others about the Good News of our Saviour Jesus Christ, who saves and gives eternal life as a free gift to all who simply believe in Him for it.

Step one: draw a cross on the inside of your thumb.
Representing Jesus Christ who died for all sinners.
Step two: Write out on the inside of your fingers S.I.N.S.
Denoting that we are all sinners. Romans 3:23.
Step three: On the backside of your hand write out B.L.O.O.D. beneath your knuckles.
Above the D on the back of your thumb draw a horizontal plane and then atop... an arrow pointing upward to the heavens.

To present this show your inner thumb and the cross and explain the death, burial and resurrection of Christ. Then wiggle your other fingers to show people/sinners. Then go over the Gospel. Lower your thumb to explain the death, lower it even more to explain the burial and then explain that we are buried with Him in baptism (Romans 6:4.) by closing your entire fist.

Now show the back of the thumb as it ascends. The D stands for "death" and the arrow represents the fact that believers are going to heaven having been raised again with Christ. Colossians 3:1-4. 2 Corinthians 4:14.

Now show the back of your fingers erected high wherein is the word: B.L.O.O.D. Explain that as saved people: all of our sins (past, present and future) have been washed away by the precious blood of Jesus. 1 John 1:7, Ephesians 1:7, 1 Peter 1:18-19. Isaiah 1:18. Never to be seen again. Isaiah 38:17.

Finish it off with a simple salvation verse: Let the listener know that because Jesus did all of this for them He has promised eternal life that can never be lost if they will believe on Him for it.

John 6:47.
*Verily, verily, I say unto you, He that believeth on me hath everlasting life.*
God bless.

# 11 – Soul-Winning with Dice

This is another way to share the Gospel with people. I tend to use this one with people mixed up under a false gospel. They are more likely to read it or listen to the presentation than an avid atheist or someone under another non-Christic religion. You need to get a singular die and then start with the 6-pipped square and thus work your way downward to the one-pipped square, each square and the number of pips has a significant meaning in propounding the gospel message.

Enjoy!

6. The word S-I-N-N-E-R is a 6-letter word describing all of us. Romans 3:23. We can't save ourselves no matter how good we try to live. Titus 3:5.

5. The 5 represents J-E-S-U-S. He is the Saviour of the world. He died for your sins, was buried and rose again to freely pay our way into heaven. John 4:42. Romans 5:8. 1 Corinthians 15:3-4.

4. G-I-F-T is a four-letter word describing eternal life. It is a free gift that God give to us by Grace. Romans 6:23. John 4:10. Romans 3:24.

3. Three represents the triune nature of God. He is three essences. God the Father. God the Son. God the Holy Spirit. 1 John 5:7.

2. Two represents the only two responses to the gospel. Believe it or don't believe it.  John 3:18. John 3:36. John 8:24.

1. One represents the One and only way to heaven! Through faith alone in Jesus Christ alone. He died for us once. Romans 6:10. We only need to be saved by simply believing on Him once. John 6:35. Once saved, always saved. John 10:28. John 5:24. Hebrews 7:25.

Consider the following verses from the Bible.

Acts 16:31.

*Believe on the Lord Jesus Christ and thou shalt be saved and thy house.*

John 14:6.

*I am the way the truth and the life no man cometh unto the father but by me.*

Jesus said:

*John 6:40.*

*And this is the will of him that sent me, that every one which seeth the Son, and believeth on him, may have everlasting life: and I will raise him up at the last day.*

God bless.

# 12 – Making Sure People Are Saved

Getting people saved is quite a simple task; getting them to have a childlike understanding of salvation can take some arduous work considering that the devil is out there confusing the minds of all people with scads of false doctrine and ideological convolution. Luke 8:12.

When giving the Gospel to people you should have a preset message ready like:

The Gospel is the Good News that God's sinless Son, Jesus Christ died for your sins, was buried and rose again to save people from hell and give them eternal life in heaven as a free gift.

John 3:16.

For God so loved the world that he gave his only begotten Son (Jesus) that whosoever believeth in Him should not perish (in hell), but have everlasting life (in heaven).

Now try to keep all the evangelistic rhetoric biblically verbatim.

Avoid trite expressions like...

1. Repent of your sins.
2. Make Christ Lord and Saviour.
3. Ask Jesus into your heart.
4. Give your life to Jesus.
5. Commit your life over to Jesus.
6. Follow Christ.
7. Obey the gospel.

Stick with Biblical words like: BELIEVE or FAITH (ALONE).

Most evangelized people will come to faith in Christ very soon after you give them a concrete gospel handout or go over the Evangecube with them or even after going over salvation verses in your Bible, the Holy Spirit makes sure of this. John 16:8-12, nevertheless Satan is still ever actively busy in snatching the truth away. Mark 4:15.

Getting people to grasp the Gospel and free grace salvation is extremely a difficult task. I've gone over the gospel excessively with children and then asked them if they were saved or what if you keep sinning after salvation just to hear a chagrining answer like: "I'd go to hell" or "I'm not saved." I've even had people ace one of my superlative gospel quizzes to weeks later not understand the doctrine of eternal security.

Here are some ways to find out if people get it or not.

Ask them if they are saved and then ask them to explain salvation back to you. Rarely someone will even have an explanation of how they got saved. Whatever answer they give go over the gospel with them again, see if their answer changes.

This shouldn't offend anyone but if it seems to just let them know that you want them to be able to evangelize so that is why you are doing this.

If you have some time to go over a few verses use this message:

Acts 16:31.

*Believe on the Lord Jesus Christ and thou shalt be saved, and thy house.*

Do you believe on Jesus? You've told me you believe so...

They should instantly reply with a "Yes."

Then ask: Are you saved? If you have believed on Jesus Christ you are saved.

Then move onto: John 6:47.

*Verily, verily, I say unto you, He that believeth on me hath everlasting life.*

Do you believe on Jesus?

Again: Yes___.

What do you have?

If you have believed on Jesus you have everlasting life like the

Bible says.

Now if it is everlasting then can you ever lose it?

Wait for their answer.

If it could be lost it isn't everlasting and has the wrong name. You can't lose it because everlasting is just that: Everlasting! It goes on forever.

A good way to make sure people get it is to give them a Bible or John's Gospel handout with dozens of verses highlighted. John 3:15, 16, 18, 36, 5:24, 6:40, 47, etc. Challenge them to read over those verses, several times if necessary.

Conclusion: it never hurts to use extreme examples especially when teaching eternal security (OSAS). The main thing one needs in finding out what someone really believes or if they really get it is to have boldness and not be afraid to do a few follow-up questions. A person's eternal destiny may be at stake to say the least and a saved mixed up new convert may confuse the Gospel and lack any conduciveness in effetely sharing the Gospel with others to say the most.

God bless.

# 13 – The Change Theory Debunked

There is a theory out there that posits that when someone gets saved they change. This is often referring to physical activity, sin in one's life, desires or just overall behavior. But is this theory biblical and true or just a theory? After reading and studying the Bible with much scrupulosity, I find it to not only be theoretical but absolutely deceptive.

Being a Christian doesn't necessarily change anything physiognomic at all. What changes is their eternal destiny and identity as the believer. John 3:18 talks about not being in a state of condemnation any longer. And in Romans 6 we read that the believer is identified with Christ by spiritual baptism.

Being born again is a supernatural act that God does and it has nothing to do with the physical or the flesh. John 6:63. 1 Peter 1:23. John 3:3-7. James 1:18. The truth is that one changes outwardly and inwardly by growth or sanctification. Psalm 119:9, John 15:5, 17:17. Isaiah 28:9-13. We grow by reading the Bible and ingesting God's transformative Word.

But this doesn't happen automatically or by sheer osmosis. In fact, a believer will not grow at all apart from personal Bible reading and walking after the Spirit. Galatians 5:25.

This takes time and discipline. But to think that this happens to every believer upon salvation is a myth and not supported by the scriptures.

The reason why this is not only fallacious but perilously deceptive is because a new convert may introspectively check his works or fruit, and after an honest assessment realize that he is not good enough and then doubt his salvation. And who wouldn't if they are honest about themselves?

With this being the case one may always turn to themselves for assurance and then the Gospel becomes one of works and not grace where one wholly relies on Christ and what He did for us (1 Corinthians 15:3-4, Romans 5:6).

Another reason why this "change theory" is so cataclysmically evil is because it forces one to make the change in order to validate that he/she is changed and this is totally a work of man no matter how much some theologian tries to convince you it is God who has divinely wrought the change.

You may hear such lies such as: before we were saved we had only one nature and now we have two natures. When in reality all we have is the old sin nature with the Holy Spirit indwelling in us.

1 Corinthians 3:16. John 7:38-39. Galatians 4:6.

The reason why I'm exposing this lie is because it actually stymies soul-winning. One may surmise that someone was a false convert because they haven't changed any whether it be a new lifestyle or attitude toward sin. But it is God that converts (Psalm 19:7, 1 Peter 1:3.) So who are we to judge whether someone's conversion was real or not?

I suspect that a false convert may be one who demands this change because that is one who hasn't trusted the finished work of Christ or hasn't simply believed in Jesus for the free gift of eternal life and is still looking to himself for proof--and this is salvation by works not by grace. And nobody is saved by their works. Titus 3:5. Romans 11:6. Galatians 2:21. The truth is a believer in Christ who has been eternally saved at the moment of faith alone in Christ alone may not bear any or much fruit for years or even decades to come. The Bible makes it clear that we will be changed in the future. 1 Corinthians 15:51-52. But if this change theory were true these verses wouldn't make any sense.

If we were changed at conversion then this futuristic change would only be a half change or an extension or continuation of the first change and not a teetotal change as the Bible says.

The main reason we should eschew this theory and abjure such a view of Christianity is because it renders false assurance and can cause Christians to neglect spiritual growth altogether. (1 Peter 2:1-2.) We look to ourselves for this so-called "change" and then we come short. Romans 3:23. And surely doubts will germinate. Either that or we just assume that all believers are changed and then we neglect Bible reading which implements real spiritual growth. 2 Peter 3:18, Matthew 5:6.

The truth of the matter is that every believer is exhorted to grow and not assume were are all just changed, when that is not the case at all.

Furthermore we should evangelize without the worriment that people are not really being converted because they don't outwardly change any. I've met too many people that put a damper on soul-winning because someone didn't "change" and asked about follow-up.

When someone talks about follow-up what they are really saying is did the person really get saved and if they did you will see some evidential fruit. The follow-up would be a means of fruit inspection. But this just shows that people are more inclined to trust in works rather than grace and that is a dangerous mentality.

We should just openly accept the fact that when a person believes on the Lord Jesus Christ for salvation (Acts 16:31,) that person is undoubtedly saved whether any kind of discernable changes take place ... at any point in time. Period. End of story.

Salvation is by grace through faith alone. Ephesians 2:8-9, not by grace plus change or grace that changes. That is a myth and a distortion of the true Gospel. We should encourage people to mature through Bible reading, prayer ... etc. (James 1:2-4,) not assume that they aren't saved because of lack of such maturity.

Conclusion. If God changed us in some physical sense then why not sinless perfection? And if the change is anything less than perfect; God is in gross error. But why would God not totally change our nature you may be wondering? Simple. He wants us to grow via reading His word. (1 Peter 2:1-2, 2 Peter

1:5-8.) And He wants us to understand that His grace is sufficient for us whether we change or not. 2 Corinthians 12:7-10.

Doing much soul-winning has sufficiently in and of itself debunked this erroneous theory. You will know after seeing drug addicts and other ranks of squalid criminals who have believed the Gospel and yet bear no (little) fruit that this theory is just a misleading hoax that Satan craftily devised. One that causes doubt, fear and self-examination, and certainly not the Gospel of Grace.

Here are some questions for the change crowd.

1. What kind of change is it?

2. When does it take place, a year from now, 10 years, two weeks?

3. How long must it last?

4. What about JW's don't they exude a changed lifestyle? Are they saved?

5. What about unsaved atheists that make positive lifestyle changes?

6. What if someone believes the Gospel and doesn't change at all?

7. Why doesn't God change us completely and not just partially considering we still frequently sin? Romans 3:23

8. What about the so-called changed Pharisee in Luke 18 bragging and even thanking God?

9. Wouldn't this so-called change cause a form of self-righteousness?

10. Why does God need us to change? Isn't the death, burial and resurrection and grace enough?

11. What about the Apostle Paul? Wasn't he acting like a so-called changed person before he was even saved?

If change had to occur upon salvation and if someone believes on Christ and doesn't change; God's word becomes a boldface lie. John 3:16, Acts 16:31, John 6:47.

**47**

Conclusion: Whether someone changes of not has nothing to do with the fact that anyone who simply believes on Jesus Christ has the free gift of everlasting life. (John 3:16.) That is the bottom line.

God bless.

# 14 – Eternal Security and Soul-Winning

Eternal security is a paramount Bible doctrine. It assures us that once a person believes on Jesus Christ for salvation they have it and always will have it no matter what they do. John 3:16. Eternal means exactly that ... eternal. Everlasting means everlasting.

That means once a person is saved they can never be lost ever again! The Bible is clear on this point. This doctrine is also called: Once saved, always saved. If one doesn't believe this not only do they make God into a liar. John 11:26, 1 John 5:9-11, 13. But they also can't properly evangelize nor can they rightly divide God's word. How can you share the Good News of the Gospel with others if it isn't really good news?

Anything less than O.S.A.S. (eternal security) is bad news and unbiblical. We should believe in eternal security because the Bible teaches it. (Hebrews 7:25. 1 Peter 1:1-5, John 10:28-30) And without this teaching we are no better than the Jehovah's Witnesses who, by the way don't believe this teaching, and just waste everyone's time with a bunch of circular jargon about the 144,000 and the so-called: 'will of God.'

So let's look at some verses that make it clear that the believer in Christ is eternally secure and that the inclusion of this doctrine in evangelism is incontestably salient. No Gospel presentation without (once saved, always saved) is the true Gospel. Any so-called gospel where this concept is bereft is another gospel as found in Galatians 1:6-9.

Before we delve into some verses on this subject, let me define what it means.

Eternal security is the immutable promise of God to the believer in Christ that no sin in thought, word, or deed can cancel, negate or take away our eternal salvation. All of our sins have been paid for so therefore salvation can never be lost or even forfeited. Once saved, always saved is true because of God's character. God cannot lie. Titus 1:2. God said eternal life was a promise. 1 John 2:25. Jesus promised everlasting life to all who have simply believed on Him for it. John 6:47. And God can't and won't go back on His Word. Psalm 89:34. Romans 11:29. James 1:17. John 10:35.

Here are some verses that affirm this wondrous doctrine.

Hebrews 9:12.
*Neither by the blood of goats and calves, but by his own blood he entered in once into the holy place, having obtained <u>eternal redemption</u> for us.*
Jesus obtained eternal redemption for us not temporary redemption--which doesn't exist. The idea that salvation could be lost would make no sense in light of this verse. Eternal anything leaves no room for loss or forfeiture otherwise it was not eternal at all.
John 10:28.
*And I give unto them eternal life; and they shall <u>never perish</u>, neither shall any man pluck them out of my hand.*
If salvation could be lost, one would certainly perish and if one perished then God lied in this verse. Never perish means just that: NEVER PERISH!
John 6:37-40.
*All that the Father giveth me shall come to me; and him that cometh to me <u>I will in no wise cast out</u>. For I came down from heaven, not to do mine own will, but the will of him that sent me. And this is the Father's will which hath sent me, that of all which he hath given me I should lose nothing, but should raise it up again at the last day. And this is the will of him that sent me, that every one which seeth the Son, and believeth on him, may have everlasting life: and <u>I will raise him up at the last</u>*

*day*.

These verses are clear. Anyone who comes to Christ by faith alone will never be cast out from Him and will be raised up at the last day which is a promise of going to heaven.

Ephesians 1:13.

*In whom ye also trusted, after that ye heard the word of truth, the gospel of your salvation: in whom also after that ye believed, ye were sealed with that holy Spirit of promise.*

The Holy Spirit has permanently sealed our eternal fate and this is a promise from God Himself.

John 5:24.

*Verily, verily, I say unto you, He that heareth my word, and believeth on him that sent me, hath everlasting life, and shall not come into condemnation; but is passed from death unto life.*

This verse in threefold proves OSAS in that it guarantees the believer a present tense possession of everlasting life, no future condemnation and an irreversible, transmigrative passage from death unto life.

Ecclesiastes 3:14.

*I know that, whatsoever God doeth, <u>it shall be for ever</u>: nothing can be put to it, nor any thing taken from it: and God doeth it, that men should fear before him.*

God saves us completely. John 3:17, 2 Corinthians 4:14, 2 Timothy 1:8-9. So therefore what God has done is forever and nothing can alter that. Eternal security!

1 John 5:13.

*These things have I written unto you that believe on the name of the Son of God; that ye may know that ye have eternal life, and that ye may believe on the name of the Son of God.*

John was writing to believers to assure them that they had eternal life and could know they had it now and because it is eternal by nature they will always have it no matter what.

If someone can read this and still conclude that salvation can be lost or forfeited they are spiritually blind and can't make sense of God's word, John 8:44-47, and they need to be evangelized all over again.

As born again Christians, we need to totally accept this doctrine and include it into our Gospel presentation for it is the quintessential heart of the Gospel. Jesus doesn't offer temporary life. The only life that Jesus has to offer is eternal life.

John 3:15.

*That whosoever believeth in him, should not perish, but have eternal life.*

The Bottom line in understanding the doctrine of eternal security is this. Salvation is based on God's grace, Ephesians 2:5, and mercy, Jude 1:21. And the Bible is clear that mercy is everlasting (Psalm 100:5) and that it endures forever. Psalm 136:1-26. We are eternally secure in Christ because God's love never runs out and the hope we have of eternal life lasts forever.

Psalm 131:3.

*Let Israel hope in the Lord from henceforth and for ever.*

God bless.

# 15 – Destroy Evil Tracts

There is a monstrous danger amid the lost that is doing more damage than the secular religions and non-Christian worldviews at large. And the culprit that I speak of are believe it or not gospel tracts--tracts I've dubbed evil--that confuse the Gospel and teach a works based salvation. 90 percent of popular tracts are teaching a false gospel.

What should we as free grace believers do about these tracts? We should thoroughly destroy them and ultimately replace them with free grace tracts.

The Bible makes it clear in 1 Peter 1:23, that there is a corruptible seed and an incorruptible seed. Sinners are saved by the incorruptible seed of the Word of God, (KJV.) So tracts that present a perverted gospel or which add anything to the Gospel are corruptible seeds that do nothing but confound the minds of those who read them. When you see a tract you should, with judicious discernment (Hebrews 5:12-14,) read over it and make sure it isn't adding any work or repentance or promise to reform ones' life to the finished work of the cross.

Below is an example of a solid free grace tract.

Are You Going To Heaven?

Here's how.
Admit you are a sinner who deserves to go to hell and can't save yourself through good works, repenting of sins, living right, obeying the commands or anything else.

Know what Jesus did for you. Jesus Christ is God's Son who came down from heaven 2000 years ago to live a perfect life of NO sin. Hebrews 4:15. He died for your sins on the cross. He was buried and rose again to freely save people from hell and give them eternal life in heaven.

Eternal life in heaven is a free gift by God's free grace. Romans 6:23. 5:18, 3:24.

We receive eternal life by simply believing in Jesus for it. Jesus promised in this Bible verse:

John 6:47.

*Verily, verily, I say unto you he that believeth on me hath everlasting life.*

According to John 6:47, if you believe on Jesus you have everlasting life.
Do you believe this? Yes_ or No_.
If you do believe on Jesus you will go to heaven no matter what. Once saved, always saved. John 5:24, John 10:26-30, John 11:26. John 6:37-40.

Notice that this tract was clear on how to be saved and gives God's all the glory whilst also upholding the simplicity of the gospel message. Now evil tracts are those that are duplicitous and rob from God's glory. Read some examples of evil tracts right at the end as they supposedly tell the lost how to be quote, unquote saved.

"Do you still want God's "wonderful plan" for your life? Great! Simply repent of (forsake) your sins, trust in Christ's sacrifice on the cross and begin to live a life of obedience to God. You must endure in Holiness to the end in order to be saved (Matt. 24:12-13). Think this world is wicked now? The worst is yet to come (Matt. 24:21) and Godly people are basically "guaranteed" to suffer (2 Tim. 3:12). BUT, you can do all things through Jesus Christ, including overcome the world (John 16:33, Phil. 4:13, 1 John 5:4-5)!"

# 16 – God Needs Us To Be Soul-Winners

Amos 3:7.

*Surely the Lord GOD will do nothing, but he revealeth his secret unto his servants the prophets.*

True. It is God that saves, John 3:17. And God gets all the glory. 1 Corinthians 1:31. And it gives God much glory for a bunch of grace-saved sinners to evangelize considering that we can do nothing without God. John 15:5. God said in His word that He has given us this job and this job is no job of mundanity but rather a divine, monolithic responsibility. The point of Amos 3:7 is to let us know that God has done everything in salvation (Psalm 24:5,) but desires that we do the evangelizing.

Look at:

2 Corinthians 5:18.

*And all things are of God, who hath reconciled us to himself by Jesus Christ, and hath given to us the ministry of reconciliation.*

Ministry of reconciliation means evangelism considering that when we tell people the gospel (1 Corinthians 15:3-4) and they believe it they are salvifically reconciled back to God. (Ephesians 2:13-17. Hebrews 10:19.)

It is a God-appointed mission for us to be Soul-Winners. Look at the following verses.

John 1:5-7.

*And the light shineth in darkness; and the darkness comprehended it not. There was a man sent from God, whose name was John. The same came for a witness, to bear witness of the Light, that all men through him might believe.*

In order for people to believe the Gospel, the light must freely shine. Matthew 5:14-16. And we must shine it constantly.

**57**

John 3:34.

*For he whom God hath sent speaketh the words of God: for God giveth not the Spirit by measure unto him.*

God sends anyone who veraciously knows His word and is diligently willing to preach it. (2 Timothy 4:2.) This isn't so with the false prophets however. (Matthew 7:15. 2 Corinthians 4:2. 2 Peter 2:1.) So it behooves us to learn it and study it wholeheartedly. (Acts 17:11. Revelation 1:3. Hebrews 5:14. 1 Timothy 4:13-16.)

Romans 10:15-18.

*And how shall they preach, except they be sent? as it is written, How beautiful are the feet of them that preach the gospel of peace, and bring glad tidings of good things! But they have not all obeyed the gospel. For Esaias saith, Lord, who hath believed our report? So then faith cometh by hearing, and hearing by the word of God. But I say, Have they not heard? Yes verily, their sound went into all the earth, and their words unto the ends of the world.*

The Holy Spirit plays a crucial role in opening the eyes of the lost. John 6:44. But we shouldn't relegate evangelistic responsibility over to Him without a collaboration.

John 16:8-11.

*And when he is come, he will reprove the world of sin, and of righteousness, and of judgment: Of sin, because they believe not on me; Of righteousness, because I go to my Father, and ye see me no more; Of judgment, because the prince of this world is judged.*

The Holy Spirit does the hard part so to speak and it is up to us to verbally preach the gospel so that salvation can be contextualized. (Isaiah 52:7, 58:1. 61:1-2. Acts 28:23.) The gospel is a free message to preach and woe unto us if we don't preach it, or distribute it, etc.

1 Corinthians 9:15-17.

*But I have used none of these things: neither have I written these things, that it should be so done unto me: for it were better for me to die, than that any man should make my glorying void. For though I preach the gospel, I have nothing to glory of: for necessity is laid upon me; yea, woe is unto me, if I preach not the gospel! For if I do this thing willingly, I have a reward: but if against my will, a dispensation of the gospel is committed unto me.*

We are commanded to preach the gospel and should obey this command at all cost.

Mark 16:15.

*And he said unto them, Go ye into all the world, and preach the gospel to every creature.*

Acts 8:4.

*Therefore they that were scattered abroad went every where preaching the word.*

Acts 5:42.

*And daily in the temple, and in every house, they ceased not to teach and preach Jesus Christ.*

In evangelism, the sky is the limit: we should give out handouts, strike up conversations, ask people what they believe or what their church believes, anything. Soul-Winning should be a 24/7 adventure. Most Christians won't do it and that is teetotal inexcusable.

My point in writing this is to render believers into Soul-Winners—not like most Christians—and to be one of the rare few that actually do what Jesus says and not just listen to Him with apathy, laziness and no spiritual motivation. Matthew 7:26.

Here is a short list of tips to help us evangelize.

1. Look affable and cordial.
2. Pray.
3. Memorize scriptures.
4. Have a small Bible handy.
5. Have clear gospel handout ready to give out.
6. Get a gospel sign.

7. Have a genuine love for the lost.

The bottom line is this: we need to spend more time evangelizing and less time trying to figure out how. The Holy Spirit will enable us anyway. See: Matthew 10:19-20.

God bless.

# 17 – Gospel Signs

A Gospel sign is basically a large, conspicuous, easy-to-make sign that has a terse but effective Gospel message on it. One in which people can and will read as it is manifestly displayed. They can be placed anywhere. I will include a list of various places to put them at the latter of this subset. Making a Gospel sign is very simple.

Print out on a standard sheet of paper with a large font size the Gospel wording of your choice. Some examples are as follows:

"Believe in Jesus Christ for eternal life."
"Jesus died for you. Believe and be saved."
"Jesus said: Whoever believes on me has everlasting life."
"He that believeth on Jesus hath everlasting life."
"JESUS SAVES."
"FAITH ALONE in CHRIST ALONE."
"Believe on the Lord Jesus Christ and thou shalt be saved."
"Believe that Jesus died to freely give you eternal life."

It is also effective to add a verse or a verse reference.
An example of how a Gospel sign might be oriented is this:

*******************
**JESUS SAVES.**
**Believe in Him**
**For**
**Eternal Life.**
**John 3:15-16.**
*******************

You can laminate them, tape them together with packaging tape and even wear them around your neck if you have a hole-puncher and some pliable string. This is a sure-kill way to get the Gospel message out without being confrontational or vocally interactive. People, for the most part, have an inveterate propensity to read monogrammed signs as they see them. Especially children who are still in the phase of learning how to read.

But does the Bible have anything to say about Gospel signs? Yes. Take a look at the following verses.

Proverbs 3:1-3.
*My son, forget not my law; but let thine heart keep my commandments: 2 For length of days, and long life, and peace, shall they add to thee. Let not mercy and truth forsake thee:* <u>*bind them about thy neck; write them upon the table of thine heart.*</u>
Proverbs 7:1-3.
*My son, keep my words, and lay up my commandments with thee. Keep my commandments, and live; and my law as the apple of thine eye.* <u>*Bind them upon thy fingers, write them upon the table of thine heart.*</u>
Proverbs 1:9.
*For they shall be an ornament of grace unto thy head, and chains about thy neck.*
This would include writing them on a sign.
Here is a list of places to put up a gospel sign.
        1. Home-doors and windows.
        2. Bathroom mirrors.
        3. Car windows.
        4. Newspaper stands.
        5. Drink machines.
        6. Telephone poles.
        7. Public trashcans.
        8. ATM machines.

9. Public restroom stalls.

10. Park benches.

11. Water fountains.

12. Trees.

13. Carwashes.

14. Bulletin boards.

15. Dumpster.

The sky is pretty much the limit.

Conclusion: a Gospel sign is always effective. Not everyone will take and read a Gospel tract or listen to a sermon, but will however read a sign—even for the sake of slaking their curiosity. There may be many debilities keeping a rookie from being an efficacious Soul-Winner and this is to be understood.

In my own personal experience I can candidly say that a Gospel sign gets the job done just the way it is. Big, bold, readable and with a powerful gospel message. (Romans 1:16.) We should keep them short, sweet and to the point, but in the same note profound enough to get the simple message out. The message that proclaims that anyone who simply believes on Jesus Christ has everlasting life. (John 6:47.)

God bless.

# 18 – Real Assurance

I've included this subset because of all the fallacious articles I've read on: The believer's assurance of salvation. In order to be an effective Soul-Winner one must have full assurance of their eternal destiny, and it must be based on the veracity of God's word and nothing else. So many people are giving false assurance or an assurance based on something as dubious as one's lifestyle as a Christian.

The problem with this is that too many 'question marks,' intervals of introspection and even self-made lies must ensue from such a faulty basis of assurance.

John's first epistle is often used in order to make a salvific assessment and this is not the point of the epistle at all. 1 John was written to strong believers (1 John 2:14) and it is to determine whether or not they are in fellowship with God. It is not a test manual to determine if one is saved or not. What determines whether one is saved or not was what they believed and what God says in His word regarding salvation. Real assurance can only be based on God's unchanging word. The tests don't work and here is why.

Look at 1 John 2:3-4.

*And hereby we do know that we know him, if we keep his commandments. He that saith, I know him, and keepeth not his commandments, is a liar, and the truth is not in him.*

False prophets try to make *knowing God* synonymous to being saved and it is not. If one is basing their assurance on whether they keep the commandments or not then there is no real assurance because no one fully keeps the commandments. (James 2:10, Romans 3:23. Galatians 3:10.) This is not about salvific assurance but is about fellowship. One would have to be kidding themselves if they used the so-called 1 John tests to determine if they were saved. What does our behavior have to do with Jesus dying and bleeding on a cruel Roman cross?

(Romans 5:10.) Another text the false brethren like to use as a so-called test of assurance is:

1 John 3:14.

*We know that we have passed from death unto life, because we love the brethren. He that loveth not his brother abideth in death.*

They base this "passage from death unto life" on whether or not they love the brethren. But this can lead to no real assurance considering that our sentiments can and will fluctuate depending how our fellow believers treat us. One may feel secure one day when everything is copasetic but what about on a bad day? Assurance must be predicated on God's immutable promises not our fickle behavior.

Let's take a look at some verses that give real assurance.

Acts 17:31.

*Because he hath appointed a day, in the which he will judge the world in righteousness by that man whom he hath ordained; whereof <u>he hath given assurance</u> unto all men, in that he hath raised him from the dead.*

According to this verse, God is the one who gives the assurance and it is based solely on the fact that He has raised Jesus Christ from the dead. When a person believes on Christ, that He died, was buried and rose again; the basis of their assurance is on the fact that Christ, through God's infinite power, arose and is seated on the right hand of God. (Hebrews 1:3, Romans 8:34.)

We should all adopt the mentality that says: God said it; that settles it!

Here are a few more verses on assurance.

Romans 4:16.

*Therefore it is of faith, that it might be by grace; to the end the promise might be sure to all the seed; not to that only which is of the law, but to that also which is of the faith of Abraham; who is the father of us all.*

This tells us that our assurance is based on God's grace, the promise that lasts to the end which proves eternal security and our faith alone in Christ alone which gave us, once and for all, an irrevocable access into God's unending grace. Romans 5:1-2.

Ultimately our assurance is based on God's Word.

Hebrews 6:11.

*And we desire that every one of you do shew the same diligence to the <u>full assurance</u> of hope unto the end.*

1 John 5:20.

*And we know that the Son of God is come, and hath given us an understanding, that we may know him that is true, and we are in him that is true, even in his Son Jesus Christ. This is the true God, and eternal life.*

This verse tells us that assurance is found in the fact that Christ already came (past tense.) Salvation is done. John 17:4. I'm so sick of people that say: "You shouldn't look back to when you first believed, you need to check and see if you are still believing and bearing fruit, etc."

Basically, they are alluding to the fact that you can't be saved the moment you believed (the first time you believed on Christ) when that is exactly when one becomes born again. (John 3:36. 1 John 5:1.) How can one look to his or herself now, when salvation took place 2000 years ago at Calvary? What these false teachers are trying to do is to get you to trust in yourself and not Christ at all—which can only lead to frustration and doubt. (Jeremiah 17:5.)

Our assurance is based on what Christ did for us, not what we do or how much faith we have or our fruit or works or whatever these heretics try to throw on you. Salvation is based on God's unchanging Word and character—nothing else.

1 John 5:13.

*These things have I written unto you that believe on the name of the Son of God; that ye may know that ye have eternal life, and that ye may believe on the name of the Son of God.*

One believes on the name of Jesus and God gives them eternal life right then and there. Moreover, He wants them knowing they have it forevermore. Pretty simple. This verse alone declares:

"God says I'm saved and going to heaven and nobody can say otherwise! NOBODY!"

This is real assurance and it is based on God's word and His word alone. In all honesty we should be so certain of our salvation we should say things like:

"If I'm not saved; NO ONE is!"

God bless.

# 19 – Soul Winning: Getting Ready – Part 1

In effective Soul-winning so much hinges around Gospel preparation and readiness. We need Bible verses memorized, Gospel tracts and other handouts and a solid illustrative presentation along with many other requisites if one is to bear evangelistic fruit. The Bible has much to say about this in Ephesians 6, the famous armor of God section of scripture. Let's take a look at what it says.

Ephesians 6:10-17.

*Finally, my brethren, be strong in the Lord, and in the power of his might. Put on the whole armour of God, that ye may be able to stand against the wiles of the devil. For we wrestle not against flesh and blood, but against principalities, against powers, against the rulers of the darkness of this world, against spiritual wickedness in high places. Wherefore take unto you the whole armour of God, that ye may be able to withstand in the evil day, and having done all, to stand. Stand therefore, having your loins girt about with truth, and having on the breastplate of righteousness; And your feet shod with the preparation of the gospel of peace; Above all, taking the shield of faith, wherewith ye shall be able to quench all the fiery darts of the wicked. And take the helmet of salvation, and the sword of the Spirit, which is the word of God.*

As we analytically read through these precious passages we see hints as to how we should arm and garb ourselves to go Soul-winning. Breastplate of righteousness, feet shod with the preparation of the Gospel of peace, the helmet of salvation and the sword of the Spirit—which is the Word of God. When going Soul-winning we need to be amply ready.

One should wear clean, business clothes to render oneself affable. You will need plenty of gospel material, an active memory of salvation verses and a handy concealable Bible to navigate through the plan of salvation when the occasion arises. I recommend getting a small zip-up pouch or a shirt with a frontal pocket to accessibly house the Gospel handouts. One can never be too ready to give someone the gospel or ask them what church they attend followed with inquiries about what they believe.

The scripture exhorts us to be able to give a veracious answer as to what we believe concerning the Gospel along with any other biblical topic.

1 Peter 3:15.

*But sanctify the Lord God in your hearts: and be ready always to give an answer to every man that asketh you a reason of the hope that is in you with meekness and fear.*

When someone asks you why they should become a Christian or something to a similar effect, you need to be able to give a profound and convincing answer. It never hurts to have a presentation contrived and quiescent in memory—and it always behooves the Soul-Winner to have something to give them with a corresponding answer.

In the next subset, I will expound how to make my preferential favorite handout, namely: a Gospel bookmark.

These are ideal for evangelism.

God bless.

# 20 – Soul Winning: Getting Ready – Part 2

One of the best Gospel handouts in my own experience are my very own gospel bookmark. You can make one easily by printing out a column of bookmarks like so. Copy and paste until the page is full.

Gospel Bookmark
God loves you.
Jesus Christ died
for you. Believe in
Him & be saved.
John 3:36. He that
believeth on the Son
hath everlasting life.
Do you believe this?
Yes_ No_.
Once saved, always saved.

To make a mass load of bookmarks one will need the following.

White or colored non-linear printing paper.
Printing ink.
Transparent tape.
A laminator.
Thermal laminating paper.
Scissors.
Rubber bands or a plastic sandwich bag.

After printing a row of bookmark-columns you will need to copy the entire row and then paste it below again and again until the page is replete with bookmarks from side to side and from top to bottom. Once the page is full, print it out. (I do so at the Public Library to save money on ink and paper.) Then, copy as many pages as you like. (I usually do about 8 to 10 sheets at a time.) Then you'll need to cut them out individually. I trim the border off first then cut them out … row by row.

Now, you will need to sandwich individual bookmarks unto the 2-fold thermal laminating paper. Place them text-side-down and tape them to the laminate for added security. After running them swimmingly through the hot laminator and allowing them to cool for a few seconds you will need to cut them out individually and then trim them meticulously. Don't trim them down to the paper but keep a small margin of plastic still exposed to ensure that they will not fall apart in the future.

You can make a firm stack of them and band them together with a rubber-band or you could just place them in a zip lock bag for safekeeping. Nevertheless you are ready to hand them out to anyone and everyone that will cordially receive them. This is very popular and effective at crowded events like festivals and holiday parties and whatnot. And the expedient thing about this is that you can easily replenish them if they run out.

I have found this method of evangelism to be effective whereupon many people have been shown a clear presentation of the gospel thereat. Once again, as I've said in many sermons, we shouldn't limited our Soul-Winning to just one or two methods. We should evangelize as the Lord leads us. (John 3:8.)

Acts 10:42.

*And he commanded us to preach unto the people, and to testify that it is he which was ordained of God to be the Judge of quick and dead.*

And If nothing else avails from this, my hope and prayer is that many people will procure these bookmarks and that the legacy of the Gospel of Grace gets passed on and on henceforth unto eternity.

God bless.

# 21 – My Doctrinal Beliefs

I hope you enjoyed the previous subsets. But in case you are wondering what I believe in other areas concerning the Bible and biblical doctrine. This sums it up.

What I believe...

***I believe in the verbal and plenary inspiration of the Bible (KJV), that the Bible is the infallible and inerrant Word of God, and the exclusive and sufficient guide for salvation, doctrine, and the spiritual life of the believer. 2 Timothy 3:16-17; 2 Peter 1:20-21.

***I believe in the Trinity, and their triune co-equality. Matthew 28:19. 1 John 5:7.

***I believe in the finished work of Jesus Christ on the cross as the unique, once and for all sacrifice for the personal sins of mankind. John 3:16 & 36; 2 Corinthians 5:21. John 19:30.

***I believe that a person receives eternal salvation by a singular moment of faith alone in Christ alone. Acts 4:12 Romans 4:5, Luke 8:50.

***I believe in eternal salvation and eternal security - "once saved, always saved." John 10:28-29. John 3:15. John 5:24.

***I believe in the universal indwelling of the Holy Spirit in every believer at the moment of salvation. 1 Corinthians 6:19. Romans 8:9.

***I believe in the sinfulness of man and his need for the personal Saviour, Jesus Christ. Acts 26:18. Ecclesiastes 7:20. Acts 16:31.

***I believe in the bodily resurrection of Jesus Christ from the grave. 1 Corinthians 15:20. John 11:25-26.

***I believe that we are in the dispensation of grace: the Church Age, and are believer-priests. 1 Peter 2:5-9.

***I believe in the pretribulation rapture. 1 Thessalonians 4:13.

***I believe in communion, prayer, Christian fellowship, and the teaching of sound doctrine. Not as requirements for salvation but because one is saved by grace and desires to grow spiritually. Acts 2:42.

***I believe in separation from those sectarian groups, churches, and organizations which violate or teach against sound Biblical doctrines. Romans 16:17.

***I believe in a literal hell that all rejecters of Christ will suffer in for all eternity.

***I reject: Calvinism in any form. Arminianism, Lordship/repentance Salvation. Catholicism, Mormonism and any other cultic religion.

Those are my basic doctrinal beliefs. Now an ancillary and personal belief I hold to is that all born-again believers in Jesus Christ should be avid and incessant soul-winners thus boldly proclaiming the gospel of grace to all people. Mark 16:15. 1 Corinthians 15:3-4. John 6:47.

God bless.

JESUS

A
V
E
S

Made in the USA
Lexington, KY
26 June 2019